Homework Book

I Love Reading

Grade 3

by
Theresa Gerig
Kris Robinson-Cobb
Glenda S. Shull

Published by Instructional Fair
an imprint of
Frank Schaffer Publications®

Frank Schaffer Publications®

Send all inquiries to:
Frank Schaffer Publications
8720 Orion Place
Columbus, OH 43240

I Love Reading—grade 3

ISBN 1-56822-828-7

3 4 5 6 7 8 9 PAT 11 10 09 08

Table of Contents

Treedale (following directions) 4–5
Sweet as Honey (summarizing) 6–7
Tad's Cereal Surprise (predicting outcomes) 8–9
Letters from Camp (Venn diagram) 10–11
Johnny Appleseed (character analysis) 12–13
Time After Time (notetaking) 14–15
Going Bowling (cause and effect) 16–17
Take a Survey (graphs and charts) 18–19
What a Mess! (classifying) 20–21
The Fire Hazard (sequencing) 22–23
Moth or Butterfly? (compare and contrast) 24–25
Whitewater Rafting (inference) 26–27
Thomas Edison (context clues) 28–29
Susie (summarizing) 30–31
Pet Show (recalling details) 32–33
Cheetahs (fact and opinion) 34–35
Squanto (main idea) 36–37
Bison (concept map) 38–39
From Tree Log to Paper Log (notetaking) 40–41
Duck-Billed Platypus (critical thinking) 42–43
Rainforests (critical thinking) 44–45
Reap What You Sow (figurative language) 46–47
The Cardinal (fact and opinion) 48–49
Sign Language (KWL) 50–51
Chocolate (taking notes) 52–53
William Wells (cause and effect) 54–55
A Nature Trail (recalling details) 56–57
Cousin Camp (classifying) 58–59
A Scavenger Hunt (following directions) 60–61
Hurricanes (drawing conclusions) 62–63
The Snake and You (compare and contrast) 64–65
Kara's Good Deed (cause and effect) 66–67
Emperor Penguins (KWL) 68–69
The Morgan Horse (paraphrasing) 70–71
Silky Webs (critical thinking) 72–73
Spring Flowers (recalling details) 74–75
Answer Key 75–80

Treedale

I am the Smith family's van. Let me tell you about my busy mornings.

From their driveway I turn north onto Apple Avenue and travel to the airport where Mr. Smith gets out.

I turn left on Chestnut Street and drive west. When I come to Oakdale I turn south. I drive until I come to the elementary school where Brittany gets out.

Still going south, I stop at the middle school where John gets out. I continue south.

When I come to Pine Path, I turn left. I travel east until I come to Maple Road. I turn north on Maple and drive to the store. I leave the store and drive north to Redbud Road. I turn east on Redbud Road and stop at the library. After the library, I turn east on Redbud Road until I come to Apple Avenue. Then I turn north and drive back home.

4

1-56822-828-7

Mark the map of Treedale with the route of the Smiths' van.
Start at the Smith family home.

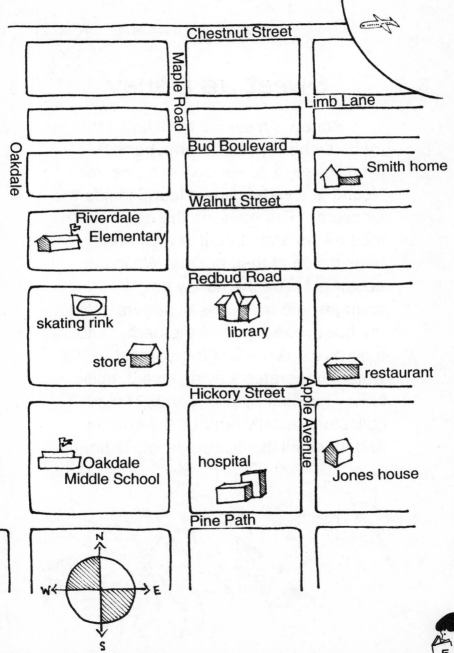

Sweet as Honey

Honey is a sweet, thick liquid that is made by honeybees. Honeybees fly from flower to flower collecting nectar. Nectar is a watery liquid found inside the blossoms. The bees sip the nectar from the flowers and store it in their honey bags inside of their bodies. While the nectar is inside the honey bag, it changes into two kinds of sugars. Next, the honeybees deposit the nectar into their hives. While it is there, most of the water evaporates leaving sweet, thick honey inside the honeycomb. Honey collectors usually remove the combs and then sell the sweet, delicious honey.

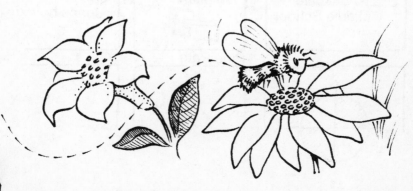

1-56822-828-7

Fill in the steps that tell how honey is made.

1. Honeybees collect nectar from flower blossoms.

2. They store it in their honey bags.

3. _____

4. _____

5. Most of the water evaporates, leaving honey in the honeycomb.

6. _____

7. _____

Write one sentence that describes how honey is made.

_____

_____

Tad's Cereal Surprise

Tad dumped the cereal from the box onto the table and poked through the flakes with his finger. He sifted through the whole pile before leaning back in his chair with a frown. There was no sports card. The advertisement on the box front claimed there was a card in every box. This box had no card.

Tad had hoped to get a card of his favorite ball player, Biff Newton, but he would have taken a card of any player. In irritation, Tad turned over the box and gave it a hard shake. To his surprise, out tumbled a tiny man in a baseball uniform. Tad blinked and stared in astonishment as the tiny man stood up and dusted himself off. He looked exactly like Biff Newton. "Thanks for getting me out of that box, kid," Biff said.

1-56822-828-7

1. What will Tad say?

_____

_____

_____

_____

_____

2. Draw what will happen next.

1-56822-828-7

Letters from Camp

Monday

Dear Mom and Dad,

Camp is no fun. I couldn't sleep last night because of the bug noise. The showers are barely warm and there are bugs in them! We have to clean our own cabins. Please, please come and get me as soon as possible.

I still love you,

Michael

Thursday

Dear Mom and Dad,

This camp is great! I am having a wonderful time. Our group has won the cabin award for three days straight! I can now ride a horse by myself and paddle a canoe through an obstacle course. We have a campfire every night and I sleep really well even though we tell ghost stories. Please, please, please don't come and get me until later. The other guys in my cabin want our parents to meet so we can plan a campout in someone's backyard before it gets too cold.

I love you!

Michael

10

1-56822-828-7

Use the Venn diagram to compare Michael's two letters. Write the number of the statements in the correct places in the diagram.

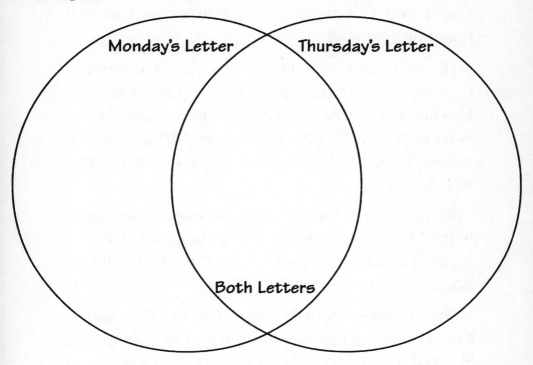

Monday's Letter   Thursday's Letter

Both Letters

1. Michael is at camp.
2. Michael is bothered by bugs.
3. Michael has made new friends.
4. Michael doesn't like the showers.
5. Michael has learned some new activities.
6. Michael doesn't like camp.
7. Michael loves his parents.
8. Michael slept well last night.
9. Michael wants to leave as soon as possible.
10. Michael writes to his parents.

1-56822-828-7

11

Johnny Appleseed

There are many tall tales about the life of Johnny Appleseed. But the facts about Johnny Appleseed may surprise you!

His real name was John Chapman. John grew up with nine brothers and sisters in Longmeadow, Massachusetts. At age 23, John began walking west with only his gun, hatchet, and knapsack. He walked over 300 miles, some barefoot, and some with shoes.

As he passed the cider mills in eastern Pennsylvania, John began gathering apple seeds. He found a piece of land and planted his first batch of apple seeds.

John traveled from Pennsylvania to Ohio, and then to Indiana planting more apple tree nurseries. He sold the young trees to settlers who used apples for apple butter, cider, and vinegar. He gave away apple trees to the poor.

As John explored, he brought not only tree seedlings but also news, stories, and books. He read to the settlers and lent them books.

In the last 20 years of his life, John was known as Johnny Appleseed. He was living in Ft. Wayne, Indiana, when he died at age 71. He left behind 15,000 apple trees and 2,000 apple seedlings for others to enjoy.

1-56822-828-7

Color the apples containing words that describe Johnny
Appleseed.

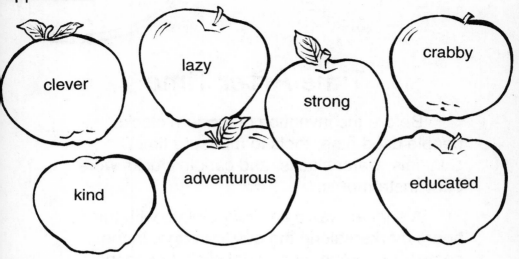

Write four sentences using four colored words from above.
The sentences should tell facts you learned about Johnny
Appleseed.

Example: Johnny Appleseed was <u>strong</u> because he
walked 300 miles.

1. _____

_____

2. _____

_____

3. _____

_____

4. _____

_____

1-56822-828-7

Time After Time

Before the invention of modern clocks, people used other tools to measure time. Sundials, water clocks, and candle clocks were early instruments.

A sundial was a flat, round plate with the hours marked along the outside edge. In the center, a gnomon, or a metal stick, lay on the plate pointing north. As the sun shone on the sundial, the gnomon created a shadow. As time passed, the shadow moved from hour marker to hour marker on the sundial. However, sundials were effective only on sunny days.

A water clock was made of a glass container with markings along the side. The water inside slowly dripped into another container. Time was measured by the amount of water remaining in the glass container.

Candle clocks were made of candles with painted bands. The bands were spaced by how much candle would burn in an hour. To measure time, the candle was lit and left to burn. The remaining bands showed how much time had passed.

14

1-56822-828-7

Complete the outline with information from the article.

A. Sundials

   1. circular flat plate with markers

   2. gnomon pointed north

   3. _____

   4. _____

   5. not effective on cloudy days or at night

B. _____

   1. _____

   2. _____

   3. _____

C. _____

   1. _____

   2. _____

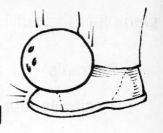

Going Bowling

Mr. League was going bowling. He loaded his bowling ball and shoes in the trunk of his car and slammed the car lid. Oops! He had locked his keys in the trunk. He went back in the house and got the spare car key. Then he unlocked the trunk.

At the bowling alley, Mr. League put on his bowling shoes. As he pulled on the shoestring, it broke. So he rented a pair of shoes.

When it was Mr. League's turn to bowl, he stepped up to the lane. Bonk! He dropped his bowling ball on his big toe. He removed his shoe to look at his toe. It was smashed and bleeding so badly that he needed to go to the emergency room.

He hobbled to the car and drove off. Suddenly a skunk walked in front of his car. Mr. League slammed on his brakes. He did not hit the skunk, but the car behind him crashed into the back of his car.

"Oh no," said Mr. League. "Now I need a tow truck for my car and a doctor for my toe."

1-56822-828-7

Draw a line from the cause to the effect.

Cause

Effect

Mr. League locked his keys in the trunk.

Mr. League had to rent bowling shoes.

Mr. League dropped the bowling ball on his toe.

Mr. League's car stopped quickly and a car hit it from behind.

Mr. League broke his shoestring.

Mr. League had to get the spare key.

A skunk walked in front of Mr. League's car.

Mr. League had to go to the emergency room.

17

1-56822-828-7

Take a Survey

Haley and Holly were third-grade students at Whispering Fields School. They were taking a survey for a school project. They needed to gather their information and present their findings to their class on a Venn diagram.

The girls decided to survey their classmates about the children in each of their families. They wanted to present this information so they could show how many classmates had just boys, just girls, or both boys and girls in their families.

Haley and Holly started by using a tally chart. This is the information they gathered.

Who is in your family?

Boys	卌 I
Girls	卌 IIII
Both Boys and Girls	卌 卌 I

1-56822-828-7

Using the key, complete the Venn diagram with the information gathered in the tally chart.

Our Classmates' Families

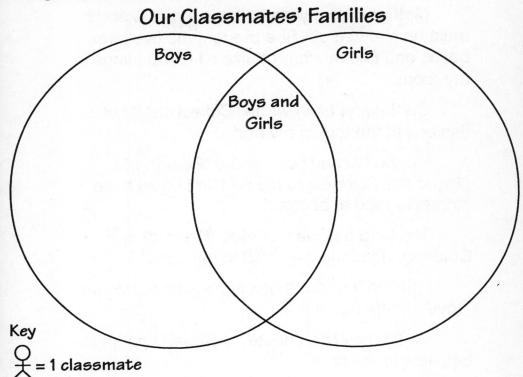

Boys

Girls

Boys and
Girls

Key

= 1 classmate

1. What does the symbol stand for? _____

2. How many classmates have only boys in their family?

_____

3. How many classmates have only girls in their family? _____

4. How many classmates have boys and girls in their family?

_____

5. How many classmates have girls in their family? _____

6. How many classmates have boys in their family? _____

7. How many classmates were surveyed? _____

1-56822-828-7

What a Mess!

Mother says my bedroom is a mess, and it must be cleaned up. She brought me five large boxes and told me to organize all of the things in my room.

On the first box I wrote "Collections." I placed this box at the foot of my bed.

On the second box I wrote "Reading." I placed this box next to my bed so I could have stories to read at bedtime.

The third box was labeled "Drawing and Coloring." I put this box next to my desk.

I placed the fourth box in my closet. I wrote "Toys" on the top of it.

On the last box I wrote "Clothes." I put this box next to my door.

Things I Found in My Room

butterfly book	comics
erasers	darts
shells	rocks and fossils
sweat pants	baseball mitt
motorcycles	leaf collection
paper	magazines
remote-control car	gloves
shoes	markers
baseball cards	pajamas
coloring books	mystery books

20

1-56822-828-7

Look at the picture of the bedroom. Label the boxes with the correct headings from the story. List the items found in the bedroom under the correct headings.

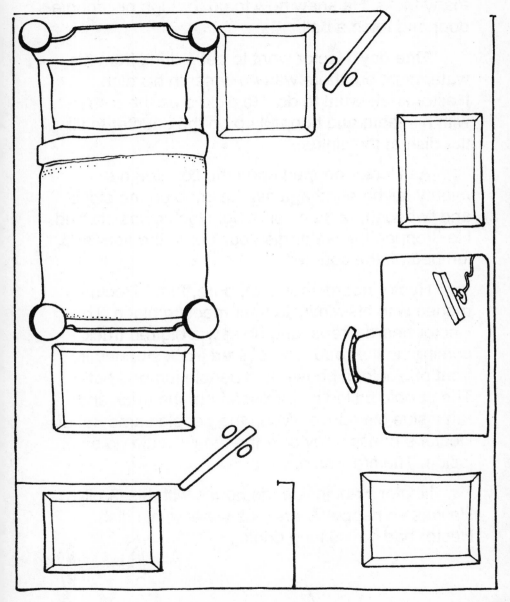

1-56822-828-7

21

The Fire Hazard

Hector was a very smart dog. He could do many tricks. He knew how to go through his doggie door and fetch a ball.

One day, Hector went to get a drink from his water dish, but there was no water in his dish. Hector knew what to do. He picked up the dish with his teeth and hopped up on the counter to fill the dish at the sink.

As Hector hopped upon the counter, his mighty tail brushed against the knob on the stove and "whoosh," a flame shot up! Hector was startled. He dropped the water dish back onto the floor and jumped off the counter.

Hector heard shouts of, "Fire, Fire!" Hector rushed with his family to their meeting place. Then Hector heard sirens, and he saw a big red truck coming up the road. The big red truck stopped in front of Hector's house, and people jumped out. The people pulled long hoses from the truck and ran inside his house. When the people came out of Hector's house, they said the family could go back inside. The fire was out.

Hector went inside the house with his family. He was so happy! There was water in his dish. Hector had a nice long drink.

1-56822-828-7

Number the statements 1, 2, and 3 in the order that they happened.

A. _____ Hector's water dish was empty.

_____ Hector's mighty tail hit the stove knob.

_____ Hector jumped up on the counter.

B. _____ Flames shot up from the stove.

_____ Hector rushed to the meeting place.

_____ Hector heard shouts of "Fire, Fire!"

C. _____ People pulled hoses from the truck and went inside the house.

_____ The family was told they could go back inside their house.

_____ Hector heard sirens and saw a big red truck coming to his house.

D. _____ He found water in his dish.

_____ Hector went back in the house with his family.

_____ Hector had a nice long drink.

1-56822-828-7

Moth or Butterfly?

Moths and butterflies are alike in many ways. They are both insects that have four wings. They both go through a metamorphosis in which they change from egg to larva to pupa and finally to an adult. Their colors may be bright and colorful or dull browns and tans.

There are some simple ways to tell them apart. Moths have thick bodies while butterflies have slender bodies. The moth's antennae are feathery. A butterfly's thin antennae look clubbed at the ends. Moths may be seen at night time. Butterflies fly during the day. While resting on a leaf or flower, a butterfly's wings are straight up. A moth rests with its wings out.

The next time you see a moth or a butterfly, will you be able to recognize it?

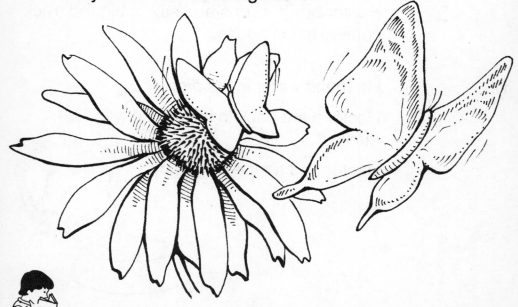

1-56822-828-7

Use the Venn diagram to compare butterflies and moths.

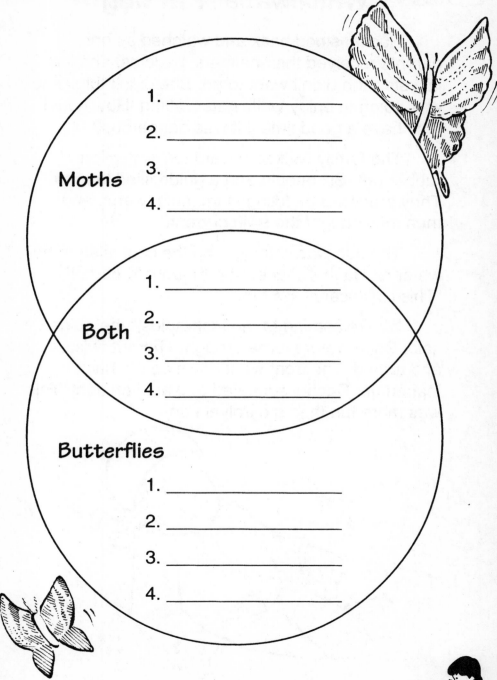

Moths

1. _____
2. _____
3. _____
4. _____

Both

1. _____
2. _____
3. _____
4. _____

Butterflies

1. _____
2. _____
3. _____
4. _____

1-56822-828-7   25

Whitewater Rafting

Rachel stood back and watched as her parents received their helmets, paddles, and life jackets. She didn't want to go. She didn't think she was going to enjoy whitewater rafting. How could they have a good time if it was dangerous?

The family walked toward the big yellow rubber raft. Six people and a guide filled the raft. They practiced paddling in the calm water, and then they caught the swift current.

The sun was shining, and the cool mist of the water hit Rachel's face. She thought to herself, "This isn't scary—it's fun."

"We're coming to the first rapids," the guide said. Calm waters turned rough. The raft twisted and turned. The front went down as the back leaped up. Rachel squealed and held on tight. This was more fun than a carnival ride!

1-56822-828-7

Answer the questions in complete sentences.

1. Why do you think Rachel didn't want to go whitewater rafting? _____

   _____

2. What clues tell you that whitewater rafting is a dangerous sport? _____

   _____

3. Why do you think a guide would be helpful when rafting?

   _____

   _____

4. Do you think Rachel enjoyed the ride? Explain.

   _____

   _____

5. Does Rachel like another activity that others would find scary? Explain.

   _____

   _____

1-56822-828-7

Thomas Edison

Thomas Edison was an inventor, a person who thinks up or makes something new. Young Thomas had a laboratory, a room for experimenting with chemicals, in the basement of his home. He continued to experiment, or try out new ideas, all of his life.

For many of his inventions, Edison was issued a patent, which gives an inventor the right to be the only person to make that product.

Some of Edison's most remembered inventions include the phonograph, the electric-light bulb, and the motion-picture camera. The phonograph is a machine that plays sounds. The sounds are stored on cylinders and flat discs, or records. The motion-picture camera can record pictures of objects that are moving. The electric-light bulb was probably the invention that helped people the most. The light bulb was cheaper to use and lasted longer than other kinds of lights. People loved Thomas Edison because his inventions made their lives better. On the day of his funeral, people across the country turned their lights off at ten o' clock. They did this to honor Thomas Edison.

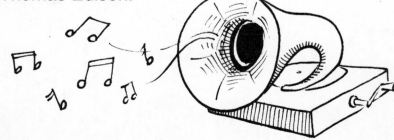

1-56822-828-7

Write the words from Edison's light bulb next to the correct meanings.

patent
inventor
records
phonograph
experiment
laboratory
Thomas Edison

_____ a person who thinks up or makes something new.

_____ a room for experimenting with chemicals

_____ It gives the inventor the right to be the only person who can make a product.

_____ a machine that plays sounds stored on cylinders or flat discs

_____ a famous inventor

_____ try out new ideas

_____ flat discs

29

Susie

In the little town of Butler, Indiana, there lived a white-tailed deer. The deer was a wild animal that enjoyed people. The people of the town named her Susie.

Susie roamed through the town visiting homes. People talked to her and fed her treats. At the school, she would stick her head in the class-room windows and let children pet her. The music teacher wrote a song about Susie. Soon the whole school was singing about her.

The town council erected a sign at each end of town. Each sign showed a picture of Susie and gave instructions for people to drive carefully. Newspapers in surrounding towns printed stories about Susie. Soon tourists came to Butler to see Susie. One spring, Susie disappeared. Everyone worried that something had happened to her. Then, after a few weeks Susie reappeared with twin fawns walking at her side. Now the town had three pets.

1-56822-828-7

Use the information in the story to complete this story summary.

The main character is _____ . She is a

_____ . Susie lived in _____ ,

_____ . Townspeople gave her _____ .

The _____ _____ wrote a song about

her. The signs in town were to warn _____ to

watch for Susie. _____ came to Butler to see

Susie. Susie returned with _____ _____ .

1-56822-828-7

Pet Show

Nathan felt sad. Tomorrow was the class pet show and he was the only student without a pet.

Nathan looked around his room. Suddenly something caught his eye. Carefully he picked it up and put it in a tin box lined with shredded newspaper. Slowly he closed the lid with a smile. Now he was ready for the pet show.

The next day at school, Nathan lifted the lid and removed the item. He held it gently in the palm of his hand.

"That's not a pet. It's just an old pink shell. It isn't even alive!" the children cried.

"Mrs. Gerig didn't say it had to be alive," Nathan said. "The word 'pet' has many meanings. One meaning is 'favorite.' This is my favorite shell. So it's my pet shell."

"Nathan is right," Mrs. Gerig said. "His shell wins the award for the "Best Behaved Pet.""

1-56822-828-7

Circle the correct detail in each sentence.

Nathan was (happy, sad) about the pet show.

Nathan used a (sack, tin box) to carry his item.

Nathan's pet was a (mouse, shell).

Nathan's pet was (brown, pink).

Nathan won a prize for the (Smallest Pet, Best Behaved Pet.)

Circle *Yes* or *No*.

Nathan's pet was alive   *yes*   *no*

Nathan's teacher gave him a prize.   *yes*   *no*

Nathan also has an animal pet.   *yes*   *no*

The word *pet* can mean *favorite*.   *yes*   *no*

     1-56822-828-7

Cheetahs

Zach loved cheetahs. He thought cheetahs were the most fascinating and beautiful animals in the world. He was working on a research paper about his favorite animal.

He read carefully through the information he had gathered. Zach wanted his research paper to be factual but also interesting. He made notes to include in his final report.

Zach was amazed that cheetahs in the wild can run up to 60 miles per hour. He had never seen them run this fast at the zoo. Cheetahs have tawny fur coats with round black spots and belong to the cat family. Zach noted that cheetah babies aren't called kittens but cubs. He thought cheetah cubs were the cutest things he had ever seen. Zach read that cheetahs are found in Africa, Southwest Asia, and India.

As Zach finished writing his report, he felt sad. He thought about the cheetahs at the zoo. Sure, they didn't go hungry, but they couldn't run free. Somehow life just wasn't the same for them as for their relatives in the wild.

1-56822-828-7

After reading about Zach's report, decide if each statement is a fact or an opinion. Write *F* for fact or *O* for opinion.

_____ 1. Cheetahs in the wild can run up to 60 miles per hour.

_____ 2. Cheetahs belong to the cat family.

_____ 3. Cheetah babies are the cutest cubs of all.

_____ 4. Cheetahs should live only in the wild.

_____ 5. Cheetahs have tawny fur with round black spots.

_____ 6. Cheetahs would make good pets.

How did Zach feel about cheetahs at the end of the story? Explain.

_____

_____

_____

_____

_____

_____

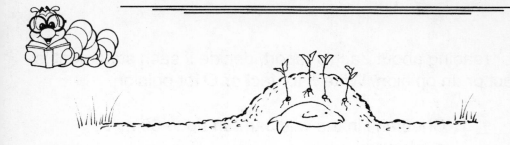

Squanto

Squanto was a Pawtuxet Indian. He lived in the area where the Pilgrims settled. Squanto learned to speak English. Squanto taught the Pilgrims many things. He helped them to live a better life in the New World.

Squanto taught the Pilgrims to plant corn. He showed them how to mound the dirt into a little hill with four or five corn seeds. He added one or two fish to the hills to give food for the corn plants as they grew. Corn became a very important crop for the Pilgrims.

Squanto also taught the Pilgrims how to find food in the wilderness. He showed them which berries and plants were safe to eat. He taught them how to spear large fish for their dinners and how to hunt wild animals.

Squanto also helped the Pilgrims communicate with other Indians. With Squanto's help, they were able to trade with one another and become friends.

The Pilgrims were lucky to have a friend such as Squanto. He helped the Pilgrims in many ways.

36

1-56822-828-7

Circle the sentence that states the main idea of the article. Number the supporting details in story order.

_____ Squanto taught the Pilgrims to plant corn.

_____ Squanto helped the Pilgrims in many important ways.

_____ Squanto taught the Pilgrims to find good berries to eat.

_____ Squanto spoke English.

_____ Squanto showed the Pilgrims how to fish and hunt.

© 2006 Frank Schaffer Publications   1-56822-828-7

Bison

Hundreds of years ago in North America, large herds of animals roamed across the continent. Some people called these animals buffalo, but they were actually bison.

Bison are mammals. The adult bison have shaggy heads with short curved horns. Their bodies are dark brown and their heads and shoulders are almost black.

Baby bison are called calves. Usually only one calf is born at a time but sometimes bison have twins. Bison calves can get up and walk soon after they are born.

Native Americans of the Plains ate bison meat and wore bison skins for clothing. They also used bison skins to cover their homes and boats. They hunted only for what they needed and used all parts of the bison.

When European settlers moved west, they wanted the bison's land for farming. They also built towns and railroads. Bison were hunted and killed ruthlessly. So many bison were destroyed that eventually there were only several hundred left.

Conservationists wanted to save the bison. They worked to get laws passed to protect them. Today bison live on farms or in parks where people can see them.

38

1-56822-828-7

Complete the concept map with information from the article.

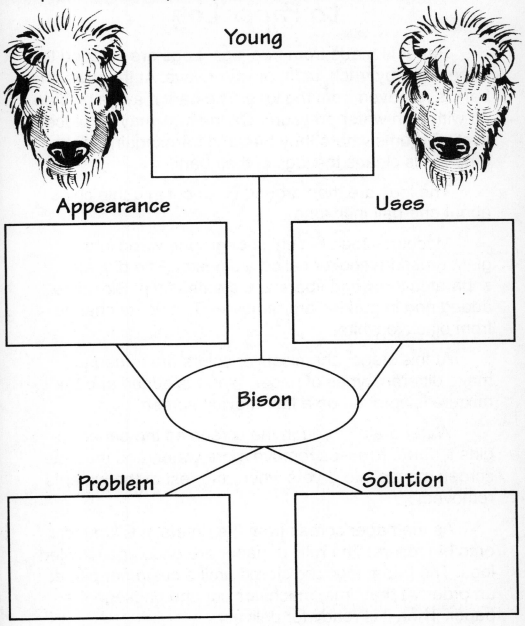

Young

Appearance

Uses

Bison

Problem

Solution

1-56822-828-7

From Tree Log to Paper Log

Paper is made from tree logs. Logs are shipped to paper mills by truck, train, or waterways. At the mills, the bark is removed from the logs. The bark may be blasted off with high water pressure. Or, the logs may be placed in steel drums where they turn and bang against each other. This cleans the logs of their bark.

The logs are then ground up or cut into thin chips about one-half inch long.

Machines feed the chips or ground wood into a giant pressure cooker called a digester. The digester separates the wood fibers and creates pulp. Bleach is added and impurities are removed. The fibers change from black to white.

At this stage, chemicals or colors are added to make different types of paper. Water is added and the mixture is sprayed on a fast-moving screen.

Water drains through the screen as the paper begins to form. Presses remove more water, and then the screen moves into dryers where the rest of the water is removed.

As the paper comes from the dryers, it is wound onto big rollers. The rolls of paper are once again called logs. The paper logs are stored until a customer places an order. At that time, machines cut and package the paper. Then it is ready for delivery.

40

                    1-56822-828-7

Complete the notes by filling in the spaces provided.

1. Logs are shipped to paper mills by . . .

   a. _____

   b. _____

   c. _____

2. Bark is removed from the logs by . . .

   a. _____

   b. _____

3. Logs are made smaller by . . .

   a. _____

   b. _____

4. A digester . . .

   a. is like a _____

   b. separates _____

5. Water is removed from the wood pulp by . . .

   a. _____

   b. _____

   c. _____

6. As the paper comes from the dryers, it _____

   _____.

7. The large rolls of paper are called _____.

8. After a customer places an order, machines

   _____.

1-56822-828-7   41

Duck-Billed Platypus

The duck-billed platypus is a strange mammal that lives in Australia and Tasmania. When it was first discovered, scientists thought it was a fake. The duck-billed platypus has the traits of a mammal. It has hair and feeds its young milk. But it lays eggs like a bird or reptile!

The platypus has soft, thick fur and a broad, flat tail like a beaver. It has a bill and webbed feet like a duck.

The platypus lives in the water. It is an excellent swimmer. It uses electrosensors in its bill to find prey. The platypus eats about a pound of worms, insects, vegetation, and shellfish each day.

When the mother duck-billed platypus is ready to lay her eggs, she makes a nest at the bottom of a long tunnel. She fills it with grass and leaves. After she lays her one, two, or three eggs, she curls around them to keep them warm.

When they first hatch, the baby platypuses' eyes are closed. Like other mammals, they cannot care for themselves. They feed on their mother's milk for five months. They are adults after a year. Platypuses live about 10 years.

1-56822-828-7

The platypus is so strange that scientists first thought it was a fake. Design a fake animal. Describe all its traits.

Animal name: _____

Animal group: _____

Outer covering: _____

Habitat: _____

_____

_____

Size: _____

Movement: _____

Feet: _____

_____

Mouth: _____

Nesting: _____

Eating habits: _____

_____

_____

Raising young: _____

Food: _____

_____

_____

Life span: _____

1-56822-828-7

Rainforests

Imagine a wonderful, green forest that is filled with plants and animals of all kinds. You have imagined a rainforest. These rainforests, found close to the equator, are warm and wet all year round. They are homes to thousands of kinds of plants, animals, and insects.

Rainforest plant life grows in layers. The top layer is the canopy. The canopy is made up of the skyscrapers of the jungle. It has the tallest trees in the forest.

The understory is thick with smaller trees, bushes, palms, and other plants. It is found under the canopy.

The forest floor is dim. Fewer plants grow because the sunlight is blocked by the upper layers of the forest.

1-56822-828-7

Label the rainforest with these words:

understory   canopy   forest floor

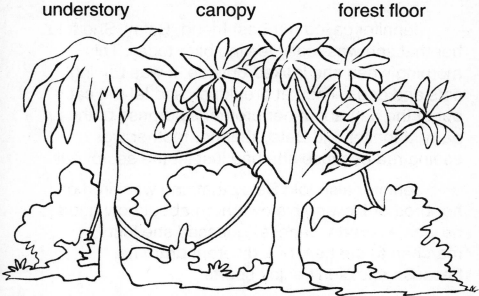

Which spot on the globe is more likely to be a rainforest?

A or B

Why would the trees in the canopy be called skyscrapers?

    a. They look like buildings.

    b. They are very tall.

1-56822-828-7

Reap What You Sow

Jennifer called her best friend, Betsy. She told her that she was really feeling blue today. This morning when she looked outside, it was raining cats and dogs. Then at breakfast, she let the cat out of the bag about her brother's surprise birthday party. Jennifer told Betsy that her mother was seeing red because she had just let the secret out.

Jennifer also told Betsy that she was tired of her brother blowing his own horn about how good he was at sports. Jennifer guessed she just marched to the beat of a different drummer because she didn't enjoy sports.

Betsy listened to her friend. She told Jennifer that she could understand why her mother was upset at her for spilling the beans about her brother's party. Betsy said that to mend some fences, maybe Jennifer should apologize to her mother and brother. Then, to put some icing on the cake, she could help out with the party.

Jennifer followed her friend's advice. Then she said she felt fit as a fiddle. Her brother's party wasn't a surprise, but it was more fun than a barrel of monkeys.

1-56822-828-7

Match the figurative language to its meaning by printing the letter next to the phrase.

_____ 1. feeling blue

_____ 2. raining cats and dogs

_____ 3. let the cat out of the bag

_____ 4. seeing red

_____ 5. blowing his own horn

_____ 6. march to the beat of a different drummer

_____ 7. spilling the beans

_____ 8. mend some fences

_____ 9. icing on the cake

_____ 10. fit as a fiddle

_____ 11. more fun than a barrel of monkeys

A. told a secret

B. really angry or upset

C. pouring down rain

D. feeling sad

E. was different from others

F. make things better

G. felt good and healthy

H. bragging about himself

I. telling something she should have kept secret

J. really good time

K. to do more than expected

1-56822-828-7

47

The Cardinal

The cardinal is a very popular bird. It is so popular it has been selected by several states to be the state bird.

Kentucky was the first state in the country to select an official state bird, and it chose the cardinal. In Illinois the schoolchildren were asked to vote on their favorite bird, and they selected the cardinal. It was also chosen to be the state bird of Indiana, North Carolina, Ohio, Virginia, and West Virginia.

The cardinal lives in many parts of the United States and Canada. The male is bright red and has a black throat and face. The female is brown with red in her wings and tail. Both male and female have a bright red crest.

At one time, cardinals were kept as pets by people who enjoyed their singing. People also used their bright feathers to decorate hats and purses. Now laws protect these birds. But their cheerful songs and bright feathers can still be enjoyed in the wild.

48

1-56822-828-7

Write *F* if the statement is a fact. Write *O* if the statement is an opinion.

_____ 1. People once used cardinal feathers as decorations.

_____ 2. The cardinal is the best bird in the world.

_____ 3. The cardinal should be the state bird in every state.

_____ 4. The male cardinal is red.

_____ 5. Both female and male cardinals have bright red crests on their heads.

Write another *fact* from the story about cardinals.

_____

_____

Write an *opinion* about cardinals.

_____

_____

1-56822-828-7

49

Important note: Before reading the article on this page, answer the first two questions on page 51.

Sign Language

Sign language is used by people who may not be able to hear or speak well. They use their hands instead of their voices to talk. Their hands make signals to show different letters, words, and ideas.

Sign language is used by other people too. Have you ever watched a football or a basketball game? The referees use hand signals to let you know what has happened in the game, such as a foul or a time out.

Have you ever been stuck in a traffic jam where there is a policeman? The policeman can use sign language to tell cars to go and wait.

Guess who else uses sign language? You! You wave your hand when you say hello and good-bye. You nod your head up and down to say "yes" and back and forth to say "no." You use your fingers to point and show which way to go. We use our hands and body to make signals all of the time!

Watch some people that you know. What kind of sign language do they use?

1-56822-828-7

Before reading "Sign Language" on page 50, answer the first two questions here.

1. Who do you know who uses sign language? _____

    _____

2. What would you like to know about sign language?

    _____

    _____

Now read the article on page 50. Then come back to this page to complete the following responses.

3. Now that you have read "Sign Language," write down everyone you know who uses sign language.

    _____

    _____

4. Look at your response to number two above. Where can you find answers to your questions? Write some possible resources here. Then go find the answers.

    _____

    _____

1-56822-828-7

51

Chocolate

Chocolate is a favorite sweet treat of many people. You may be surprised to learn that chocolate comes from a cacao bean, which is a bitter seed that grows on a tree.

The cacao tree grows in warm climates. Most cacao trees are found in West Africa. The trees reach the height of 25 feet tall. The fruit of the cacao tree looks like a pod and grows in all seasons. When it is ripe, the pod may be red, yellow, or green. The pod is filled with seeds, also known as cacao beans.

The seeds are processed by the growers. The seeds are scooped out of the ripe pods and left to ferment underneath burlap or banana leaves. After about a week and a half, the fermented beans are left in the sun to dry. Next, the cacao beans are bagged up and shipped to chocolate manufacturers.

Chocolate manufacturers make chocolate through a complicated process. They clean the beans and take the shells off. They also roast the beans and grind them to produce a liquid chocolate. To make the chocolate that we like to eat as candy, manufacturers must add sugar and milk.

52

1-56822-828-7

After reading the article on chocolate, complete the outline to take notes on your reading.

I Chocolate starts on the cacao tree.

   A. The cacao tree

     1. _____

     2. _____

     3. _____

   B. The cacao fruit

     1. _____

     2. _____

II From tree to beans

   A. Cacao seeds are processed by the growers.

     1. _____

     2. _____

     3. _____

   B. The beans are bagged and sent to chocolate manufacturers.

III Making chocolate

   A. _____

   B. _____

   C. _____

William Wells

Long ago, a boy named William Wells lived with his family in Kentucky. When he was about eleven years old, William was kidnapped and brought to Indiana where he was taken to the village of Little Turtle, chief of the Miami Indians.

The Miami people admired William's strength and knew he would be a good warrior. He was adopted by a family and given the name Apakonit, which means wild carrot.

William was taught the ways of the Miami people. He learned to hunt, shoot, and use a tomahawk. William became the adopted son of Chief Little Turtle and fought with Little Turtle in many battles.

During these battles, William killed many American soldiers. He wondered if some of these soldiers were his relatives. William returned to Kentucky to visit his family. There, he took a job as a scout for the American soldiers.

William loved both the white people and the Miami people. He remained friends with Little Turtle and worked with the chief to help bring peace between the two peoples.

1-56822-828-7

Match the cause and effect. Write a letter before each
numbered sentence.

_____ 1. William Wells
traveled from
Kentucky to
Indiana.

_____ 2. William was
adopted by a
Miami family.

_____ 3. William returned
to Kentucky.

_____ 4. William worked
to bring peace
between the two
peoples.

a. He wanted to visit
his family.

b. He loved the white
people and the Miami
people.

c. He was kidnapped and
taken to Little Turtle's
village.

d. The Miami people knew
William would be a
good warrior.

A Nature Trail

Michael and Jim stood near the naturalist at the front of the group. They wanted to hike the guided trail to learn what they could about the flowers and other plants in the local state park.

The naturalist explained that tourists weren't allowed to pick the flowers. If everyone who hiked the trail picked just one flower each, soon no flowers would be left for the remaining tourists to enjoy.

Just a few steps down the trail, the naturalist stopped by some tall orange flowers. She told the group that people call these flowers tiger lilies because of their orange and black colors. Others call them day lilies because they have blossoms on sunny days.

The group continued down the trail. They learned about other flowers. They learned that a small butter-colored flower with a cup shape was called a buttercup. A flower with bright yellow petals and a black center was the blacked-eyed daisy, or black-eyed Susan.

The naturalist pointed to a white, lacy flower. This, she told the group, was wild carrot and they could eat the roots just as Native Americans had many years ago. She added that it was best known as Queen Anne's lace.

She pointed out other flowers and plants of interest, such as yarrow, wild blueberries, ferns, and thistle. Just as they neared the end of the trail, the naturalist pointed to some wide green leaves clustered together. She explained that this "cabbage" was named for its smell. We couldn't smell anything until she broke a leaf in two,

1-56822-828-7

and then we scattered. We said good-bye as the naturalist explained, "This plant is called skunk cabbage!"

After reading "A Nature Trail," answer the questions below.

1. Where did the boys go hiking?

   _____

   _____

2. Why did the boys take a guided tour instead of going by themselves?

   _____

   _____

3. Why shouldn't the boys pick the flowers?

   _____

   _____

4. What is another name for the tiger lily? Why is it called this? _____

   _____

5. What plant did Native Americans use? How did they use this? _____

   _____

6. What kind of cabbage did the naturalist show the group? Why do you think they scattered?

   _____

   _____

1-56822-828-7   57

Cousin Camp

Randy, Kathi, Doug, Jodi, Janet, and Max went to camp together every summer. Camp lasted five days, and it was great fun. The best part was that the counselors were their grand-parents! Every year of cousin camp was different. One year, they went camping at a campground. The cousins hiked, fished, swam, and rode bikes together. At night, they roasted hot dogs and marshmallows over an open fire. They fed the raccoons that came out at night.

Another year, the cousins traveled in the counselors' big van. The cousins visited museums and historic sites and ate hot dogs at a baseball game. They stayed in two hotel rooms with connecting doors.

One year, the counselors held camp at their house. The cousins baked cookies, played games, painted, and made craft projects. The counselors had a scavenger hunt in the afternoon. When it was really hot, they took the campers to the city pool or local movie theater to keep cool. The best night was the slumber party. Sleeping bags, pizza, popcorn, and soda pop were brought to the family room where the cousins watched videos late into the night.

Cousin Camp is great fun. There is only one requirement—you have to be a cousin to go!

1-56822-828-7

Refer to the Word Bank to list the correct activities under each year at Cousin Camp.

Word Bank

crafts and games	movie theater	museums
baseball park	slumber party	hotel
hiking	baked cookies	rode bikes
historic sites	fishing	van ride
roasted hot dogs	marshmallows	pizza
connecting rooms	raccoons	videos

Cousin Camp at the Campground

_____

_____

_____

_____

_____

_____

Traveling Cousin Camp

_____

_____

_____

_____

_____

_____

Cousin Camp at the Counselors' Home

_____   _____

_____   _____

_____   _____

1-56822-828-7

59

A Scavenger Hunt

Melvin and his friends went on a scavenger hunt. They split into two teams and left from his house at the same time. On page 61, read about the path each team took. Trace their routes on the map with a blue crayon and red crayon. Draw the item found at each location.

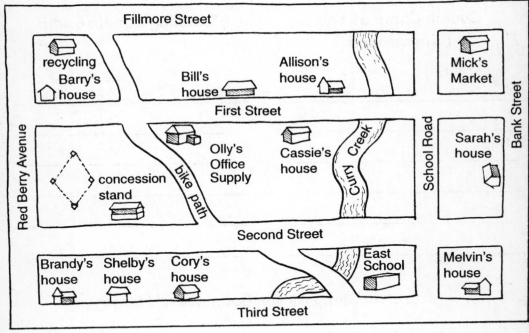

© 2006 Frank Schaffer Publications   1-56822-828-7

Red Team

1. From Melvin's house, the red team rode their bikes west on Third Street. They found a paper clip in the parking lot of East School.
2. They rode northwest on the bike path and turned left on Second Street. They got a paper bag from the concession stand.
3. They continued west on Second Street and rode north on Red Berry Avenue. They stopped at Barry's house and got a sock with a hole in it.
4. The team rode north on Red Berry Avenue and turned right on Fillmore Street. They found an old newspaper at the recycling drop-off station,
5. Next, the team rode east on Fillmore Street to Mick's Market. Mick gave them a blue rubber band.
6. They rode south on Bank Street to Sarah's house. Sarah's mom gave them an empty soup can.
7. The boys returned to Melvin's house. Their trip took 20 minutes.

Blue Team

1. The blue team left Melvin's and rode north on Bank Street to Sarah's house. Sarah's mom gave them a sock with a hole in it.
2. They continued north on Bank Street and turned left on First Street. They crossed Curvy Creek to Cassie's house. Cassie's dad gave them a blue rubber band.
3. They crossed the street to Allison's house but no one was home, so they rode to Bill's. Bill's sister gave them an old newspaper.
4. The team rode west to Olly's Office Supply. There they got a paper clip and a small paper bag.
5. Next they rode west on First Street. They turned south on Red Berry Avenue and rode to the end of the street.
6. The boys turned east on Third Street and picked up a soup can from Brandy's mom.
7. They returned to Melvin's house. Their trip took 15 minutes.

1-56822-828-7

61

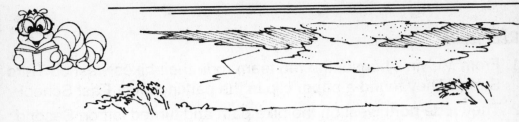

Hurricanes

Hurricanes are among the largest and most dangerous storms on Earth. Hurricanes can cause damage to homes or destroy whole cities.

Meteorologists, or weather scientists, closely track storms that form on the oceans. They watch to see if these storms grow bigger and stronger. They watch to see if they will become hurricanes.

Hurricanes are given names by a group of meteorologists. They use an alphabetical list of male and female names. The first hurricane of the year is given a name beginning with the letter A. If it is female, the next hurricane that same year will be a male name that begins with B. The next hurricane will be a female name that begins with C. The naming will continue using this pattern. There are no hurricane names that begin with Q, U, X, Y, or Z.

Scientists use these names to report information about certain hurricanes. Thankfully, scientists have not had to use all 21 names in one year.

1-56822-828-7

Write the answers to these questions.

1. Why do you think meteorologists track storms?

   _____

   _____

2. Why do you think there are there only 21 letters to name hurricanes rather than the 26 letters of the alphabet?

   _____

   _____

3. Why is it good that scientists have not used 21 names in one year?

   _____

   _____

4. Why do you think meteorology is an important job?

   _____

   _____

5. Imagine you are a member of a group who is choosing names for hurricanes. Use the pattern described in the article to complete this list of names.

1. Ashley	8. _____	15. _____
2. Bob	9. _____	16. _____
3. _____	10. _____	17. _____
4. _____	11. Katie	18. _____
5. _____	12. _____	19. _____
6. Freddy	13. _____	20. Victor
7. _____	14. _____	21. _____

1-56822-828-7

The Snake and You

Have you ever been surprised by a snake crossing your path? Perhaps you were afraid because snakes are very different from you and I.

Most snakes begin life inside an egg. As the baby snake grows larger inside the egg, the leathery eggshell expands. When it is ready to hatch, the snake breaks the shell with a special tooth on its nose. The egg tooth is shed when the snake emerges from the shell.

The snake grows quickly when it is young. Its skin does not grow. The snake sheds its old skin by crawling out of it and leaving it whole. Snake eyes are protected by a clear film. A snake never closes its eyes because it has no eyelids. The snake also has no outer ears.

Most snakes eat birds, mice, frogs, fish, lizards, and rabbits. The snake does not chew its food but swallows it whole. After the snake is full, it may not eat again for several weeks.

Snakes are helpful to humans because they eat animals we think of as pests. So, if a snake crosses your path, thank it for its hard work.

1-56822-828-7

Put an *X* in the boxes that describe how snakes and humans are alike. Put an *O* in the boxes that describe snakes only.

have skin	they eat	do not chew their food
shed old skin in one piece	hatch out of eggs	do not eat for weeks
have no eyelids	they grow	swallow their food

Draw a line through the three in a row. Who wins the tic-tac-toe game?

Are humans much like snakes? Explain. _____

_____

_____

_____

1-56822-828-7

Kara's Good Deed

Kara couldn't sleep. She thought she heard someone crying downstairs. She tiptoed downstairs to check things out.

As Kara turned on the light, she saw a tiny figure sitting beside a spilled vase of flowers on the table.

Kara could see it was a fairy that had been crying. She quietly asked what was wrong. The fairy explained that she had been resting in a flower in the garden with her fairy sister when Kara's mother picked the flower and brought it and her inside.

Kara picked up the dainty fairy and went outside. She walked to the flower garden in the moonlight. Kara held her hand open, and her tiny friend flew to the flowers. Kara heard joyous cries as the fairy returned to her sister.

Kara hurried inside. She cleaned up the overturned vase and set the flowers in fresh water back in the middle of the table. Then she went to bed.

Kara quickly fell back to sleep. She never knew that two fairy sisters sprinkled happy dust outside her window.

1-56822-828-7

Answer the following questions.

1. What caused Kara to awaken? _____

_____

2. What effect did picking flowers have on the fairy?

_____

_____

3. What do you think caused the vase and flowers to
   turn over?

_____

_____.

4. What caused Kara to go to the flower garden in the

   moonlight? _____

_____

5. What effect do you think the happy dust will have on

   Kara? _____

_____

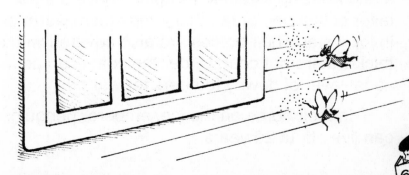

Before reading "Emperor Penguins," complete the first two parts of the chart on page 69.

Emperor Penguins

The emperor penguin is the largest of all the penguins. The adult stands about 3 feet 9 inches tall and weighs around 90 pounds. It has jet-black feathers covering its head and back. The penguin's front is dazzling white. Yellow patches mark the sides of its head and throat. Its beak is red and purple.

Emperor penguins breed differently than other penguins. The female lays one egg and passes the responsibility of care for the egg to her partner. The male keeps the egg warm by placing it on his feet below his belly. He stands like this for two months without eating. When the egg hatches, the female cares for the chick and the father gets some food and sleep.

Since it is very cold in Antarctica where penguins live, their bodies must be able to with-stand freezing weather. Penguins have a thick layer of blubber, or fat, that keeps them warm even in icy water. Their bodies are also covered with a thick waterproof coat. Under the coat is an addi-tional layer of downy feathers for warmth.

In their home on the ice, emperor penguins can live about 20 years.

1-56822-828-7

What I know about penguins

What I want to know

What I learned from reading

1-56822-828-7

The Morgan Horse

1. The Morgan Horse is a popular breed of horse. Many people own Morgan horses because they are fast, hard-working, and gentle.

2. The first Morgan was a small, reddish-brown horse with a soft and glossy coat. His name was Figure. Figure was owned by a man named Justin Morgan.

3. When Justin Morgan died, Figure was given away and his name was changed to Justin Morgan. Justin Morgan was put to work pulling heavy loads. He could pull loads that bigger horses could not pull.

4. Justin Morgan was also very fast. His legs were short, but he could outrun most of the racehorses in his area. He became famous for his speed and strength.

5. Justin Morgan was the father of many colts. His colts looked very much like him. The colts and their offspring were all known as Morgan horses. There are many Morgan horses today. Like the first Morgan horse, they are gentle and hard-working.

          1-56822-828-7

Read the story. Fill in the circle in front of the sentence that best paraphrases each numbered paragraph in the story.

1. ○ There are many people and many Morgan horses.

   ○ Morgan horses are popular because they have good characteristics.

2. ○ Justin Morgan owned a reddish-brown horse named Figure.

   ○ All horses have a mane and tail.

3. ○ The hard-working horse was renamed Justin Morgan.

   ○ Figure ran away from Justin Morgan pulling a heavy load.

4. ○ Justin Morgan became famous because he could outrun and outpull most horses.

   ○ Justin Morgan became a famous trick horse.

5. ○ Colts are young horses.

   ○ There are many Morgan horses today, and they are like Justin Morgan.

1-56822-828-7

71

Silky Webs

Spiders can make different kinds of webs from the silk they spin. By looking at the kinds of webs, you may be able to tell the kind of spider that made it.

Tangled webs are made by house spiders and black widows. These webs of tangled silk are used to trap insects. When an insect gets caught, the spider will have its meal.

Sheet webs are made by platform spiders. These webs are found in tall grass or in the branches of trees or shrubs. They look like flat sheets. A spider hides under the sheet to wait for an insect. Then it quickly pulls its catch through the webbing.

The triangle web looks like a triangle. The triangle spider traps insects in its sticky strands.

Yellow garden spiders spin orb webs that are shaped like circles. This beautiful pattern of circles inside circles can be deadly for careless insects.

1-56822-828-7

Under each web, write the name of the spider that might
weave it. Write the names of the webs above the illustrations.

Web: _____

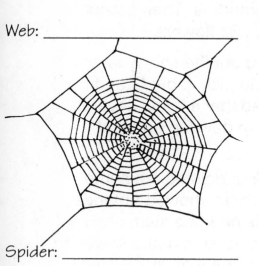

Spider: _____

Web: _____

Spider: _____

Web: _____

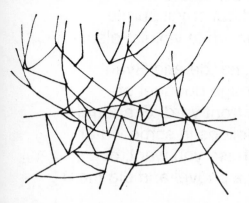

Spider: _____

Web: _____

Spider: _____

1-56822-828-7

73

Spring Flowers

Amanda and Ryan went for a hike in the marshy woods with their grandma. Their grandma loved to teach them about wild flowers.

First Grandma pointed out the showy lady's slipper. Ryan reached out to pick it, but Grandma stopped him. She explained that it takes several years for a flower like that to develop and that it was best to leave it alone.

As they hiked, Grandma pointed out some green umbrella-like plants. She showed Amanda and Ryan how some plants had one stem and no flower, but the two-stemmed plants had a flower. In May, the small white flower drops off and a small fruit develops. The fruit smells like an apple so it's called a May apple. Amanda and Ryan looked at lots of the plants to see if they had a flower, but they didn't pick any.

At the edge of the woods, Grandma knelt in a carpet of green and pointed out small purple violets. Amanda found some white violets, also.

Later that afternoon, Amanda and Ryan surprised Grandma with a huge bouquet of dandelions picked from the front yard. Grandma smiled as she put the dandelions in some water. She told them, "Pick all of these you want, or better yet, ask Grandpa for a shovel and dig them up by the roots!"

 1-56822-828-7

Answer the questions below in complete sentences.

1. Who went hiking? _____

_____

2. Where did the hikers hike? _____

_____

3. Why didn't Grandma want Ryan to pick the showy lady's

slipper? _____

_____

_____

4. How does the May apple get its name? _____

_____

_____

5. Why do you think Grandma said it was okay to pick the

dandelions? _____

_____

_____

_____

Answer Key

Treedale

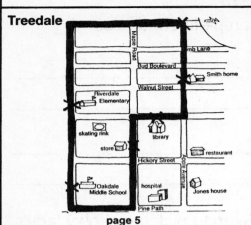

page 5

Sweet as Honey

1. Honeybees collect nectar.
2. They store it in their honey bags.
3. The honey changes into two kinds of sugars.
4. The honeybees deposit the nectar into their hives.
5. The water evaporates
6. Honey collectors remove the combs.
7. They sell the honey.

page 7

Tad's Cereal Surprise

Predictions will vary.

page 9

Letters from Camp

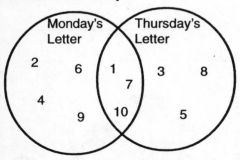

page 11

Johnny Appleseed

Color the apples containing the following words: *adventurous, strong, kind, educated, clever*

Sentences will vary.

page 13

Time After Time

A. Sundials
  3. gnomen creates a shadow
  4. The shadow moves as time passes, marking the hours.

B. Water Clocks
  1. glass container with markings
  2. water drips into a second container
  3. Time is measured by the amount of water remaining.

C. Candle Clocks
  1. made of candles with painted bands
  2. To measure time, the candle is lit and left to burn. The remaining bands show elapsed time.

page 15

Going Bowling

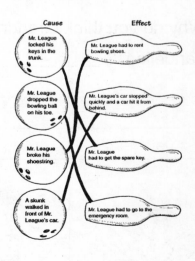

page 17

                    1-56822-828-7

Take a Survey

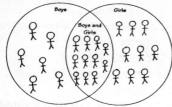

1. 1 classmate
2. 6
3. 9
4. 11
5. 20
6. 17
7. 26

page 19

What a Mess!

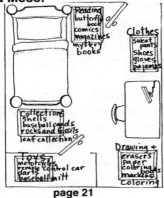

page 21

The Fire Hazard

A. 1 3 2
B. 1 3 2
C. 2 3 1
D. 2 1 3

page 23

Moth or Butterfly?

Moths
1. thick bodies
2. feathery antennae
3. seen at night
4. rests with its wings out

Both
1. insects
2. four wings
3. go through a metamorphosis

4. colors range from browns and tans to bright and colorful

Butterflies
1. slender bodies
2. thin, clubbed antennae
3. fly during the day
4. rests with wings straight up

page 25

Whitewater Rafting

1. She stood back and worried about the danger.
2. They must wear helmets and life jackets.
3. A guide may teach about the exciting and dangerous parts and how to handle the raft.
4. Yes, she squealed.
5. carnival rides

page 27

Thomas Edison

inventor
laboratory
patent
phonograph
Thomas Edison
experiment
records

page 29

Susie

The main character is Susie. She is a deer. Susie lived in Butler, Indiana. Townspeople gave her treats. The music teacher wrote a song about her. The signs in town were to warn drivers to watch for Susie. Tourists came to Butler to see Susie. Susie retruned with twin fawns.

page 31

Pet Show

1. sad	no
2. tin box	yes
3. shell	
4. pink	no
5. Best Behaved Pet	yes

page 33

Cheetahs

1. F	4. O	Paragraphs
2. F	5. F	will vary.
3. O	6. O	

page 35

Squanto

Main Idea: Squanto helped the Pilgrims in many important ways.

3
2
4
1
5

page 37

Bison

Young: called calves, one born at a time, can walk soon after birth

Appearance: shaggy heads, short curved horns, dark brown bodies, black heads

Uses: eat their meat; skins used for clothing, homes, and boats

Problem: European settlers hunted and killed ruthlesssly. Only several hun dred were left.

Solution: Laws were passed to protect bison. Bison live on farms or in parks.

page 39

From Tree Log to Paper Log

1. truck, train, waterways
2. blasted off with water or banged off in steel drums
3. ground up or cut into thin chips
4. like a pressure cooker; separates the wood fibers
5. drains on screens, presses remove more water, dryers remove the last
6. wound on big rollers
7. logs
8. cut and package the paper

page 41

Duck-Billed Platypus

Animal inventions will vary.

page 43

Rainforests

Treetops should be labeled *canopy*.
Thick bushes are the *understory*.
The ground is the *forest floor*.

B is closest to the equator.

b. They are very tall.

page 45

Reap What You Sow

1.	D	7.	I
2.	C	8.	F
3.	A	9.	K
4.	B	10.	G
5.	H	11.	J
6.	E		

page 47

The Cardinal

1.	F	Facts and opinions will
2.	O	vary.
3.	O	Fact: The cardinal is the
4.	F	state bird of Virginia.
5.	F	Opinion: Cardinals have
		beautiful feathers.

page 49

  1-56822-828-7

Sign Language

1. Answers will vary.
2. Answers will vary.
3. In addition to people who use American sign language, there are referees, policeman, and anyone who waves or gestures
4. Answers will vary.

page 51

Chocolate

I
A. 1. Grows in warm climates
   2. Found in West Africa
   3. As tall as 25 ft.
B. 1. Is a yellow, green, or red pod
   2. Pod is filled with seeds
II
A. 1. Seeds scooped out of pods
   2. Left to ferment under burlap
   3. Dried in the sun
III
A. Clean and shell the beans
B. Roast and grind the beans
C. Add sugar and milk

page 53

William Wells

1. c
2. d
3. a
4. b

page 55

A Nature Trail

1. at the local state park
2. They wanted to learn about the flowers and plants.
3. If everyone did, there would be no flowers left.
4. Day lilies; because they have blossoms on sunny days.
5. Wild carrot; they ate the roots.
6. Skunk cabbage; it smelled bad.

page 57

Cousin Camp

Campground: hiking, roasted hot dogs, fishing, rode bikes, marshmallows, raccoons

Traveling: van ride, museums, historic sites, baseball park, hotel, connecting rooms

Counselors' home: baked cookies, crafts and games, movie theater, slumber party, pizza, videos

page 59

A Scavenger Hunt

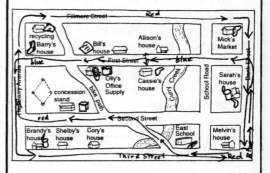

page 61

Hurricanes

1. They can predict the coming of a storm.
2. Some letters are not used because not many names begin with those letters.
3. There have not been that many storms.
4. Meteorologists can warn people of dangerous storms so they can take shelter.
5. Names will vary, but should alternate male female and be in alphabetical order. No names should be given for the letters Q, U, X, Y, or Z.

page 63

The Snake and You

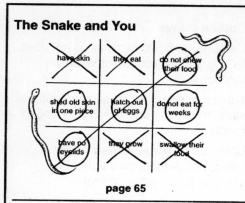

page 65

Kara's Good Deed

1. She heard someone crying.
2. The fairy was taken away from her sister.
3. The fairy probably tipped it over.
4. She was returning the fairy to her sister.
5. Answers will vary. She will probably be very happy. Good things may happen to her.

page 67

Emperor Penguins

KWL charts will vary.

page 69

The Morgan Horse

1. Morgan horses are popular because they have good characteristics.
2. Justin Morgan owned a reddish-brown horse named Figure.
3. The hard-working horse was renamed Justin Morgan.
4. Justin Morgan became famous because he could outpull and outrun most horses.
5. There are many Morgan horses today, and they are like Justin Morgan.

page 71

Silky Webs

Orb web
yellow garden spider

Triangle web
triangle spider

Tangled web
house spider
black widow

Sheet web
platform spider

page 73

Spring Flowers

1. Amanda and Ryan and their grandma
2. in the marshy woods
3. It takes several years for a plant like it to grow. It is best to leave it alone.
4. The fruit of the flower smells like an apple.
5. Dandelions are considered weeds. They grow quickly and spread over lawns. Grandma probably doesn't want them in her yard.

page 75